DRAWING DINOSAURS

DRAWING PLESIOSAURUS

AND OTHER OCEAN DINOSAURS

STEVE BEAUMONT

PowerKiDS
press.

New York

Published in 2010 by The Rosen Publishing Group, Inc.
29 East 21st Street, New York, NY 10010

Copyright © 2010 Arcturus Publishing Ltd

Artwork and text: Steve Beaumont
Editor (Arcturus): Carron Brown
Designer: Steve Flight

Library of Congress Cataloging-in-Publication Data

Beaumont, Steve.
  Drawing Plesiosaurus and other ocean dinosaurs / Steve Beaumont. — 1st ed.
      p. cm. — (Drawing dinosaurs)
  Includes index.
  ISBN 978-1-61531-903-9 (library binding) — ISBN 978-1-4488-0426-9 (pbk.) —
ISBN 978-1-4488-0427-6 (6-pack)
  1. Dinosaurs in art—Juvenile literature. 2. Drawing—Technique—Juvenile literature.
  3. Plesiosaurus—Juvenile literature. I. Title.
  NC780.5.B393 2010
  743.6—dc22
                                    2009033266

Printed in China

CPSIA compliance information: Batch #AW0102PK : For further information contact Rosen Publishing, New York, New York at 1-800-237-9932

CONTENTS

"Dinosaurs"… the word conjures up all kinds of powerful and exciting images. The word "dinosaur" is often used to describe all prehistoric reptiles, but not all were true dinosaurs. Plesiosaurus, Ichthyosaurus, and Liopleurodon were ocean reptiles and so were not true dinosaurs. One feature that separated the reptiles from the dinosaurs was the structure of their limbs. Dinosaurs had limbs which allowed them to stand upright.

These amazing creatures ruled Earth for over 160 million years until, suddenly, they all died out. No one has ever seen a living, moving, roaring dinosaur, but thanks to the research of paleontologists, who piece together dinosaur fossils, we now have a pretty good idea what many of them looked like.

Some were as big as huge buildings, others had enormous teeth, scaly skin, horns, claws, and body armor. Dinosaurs have played starring roles in books, on television, and in blockbuster movies, and now it's time for them to take center stage on your drawing pad!

In this book we've chosen three incredible ocean dinosaurs for you to learn how to draw. We've also included a prehistoric ocean landscape for you to sketch, so you can really set the scene for your drawings.

You'll find advice on essential drawing tools, tips on how to get the best results, and easy-to-follow step-by-step instructions showing you how to draw each dinosaur. So, it's time to bring these extinct monsters back to life— let's draw some dinosaurs!

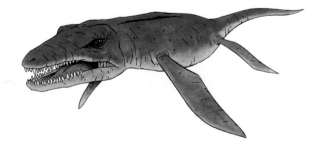

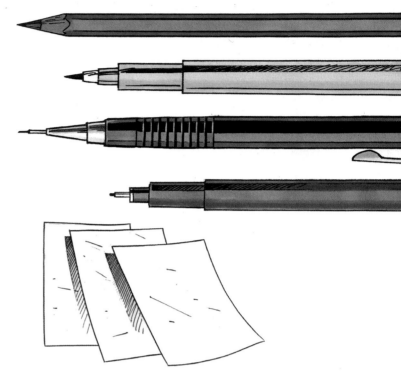

DRAWING TOOLS

Let's start with the essential drawing tools you'll need to create awesome illustrations. Build up your collection as your drawing skills improve.

LAYOUT PAPER

Artists, both as professionals and as students, rarely produce their first practice sketches on their best quality art paper. It's a good idea to buy some inexpensive plain letter-size paper from a stationery store for all of your practice sketches. Buy the least expensive kind.

Most professional illustrators use cheaper paper for basic layouts and practice sketches before they get to the more serious task of producing a masterpiece on more costly material.

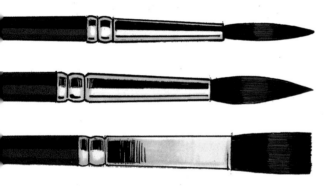

HEAVY DRAWING PAPER

This paper is ideal for your final version. You don't have to buy the most expensive brand—most decent arts and crafts stores will stock their own brand or another lower-priced brand and unless you're thinking of turning professional, these will work fine.

WATERCOLOR PAPER

This paper is made from 100 percent cotton and is much higher quality than wood-based papers. Most arts and crafts stores will stock a large range of weights and sizes—140 pounds per ream (300 g/sq m) will be fine.

LINE ART PAPER

If you want to practice black and white ink drawing, line art paper enables you to produce a nice clear crisp line. You'll get better results than you would on heavier paper as it has a much smoother surface.

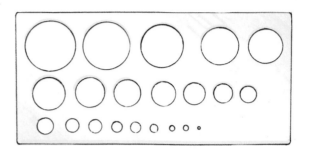

PENCILS

It's best not to cut corners on quality here. Get a good range of graphite (lead) pencils ranging from soft (#1) to hard (#4).

Hard lead lasts longer and leaves less graphite on the paper. Soft lead leaves more lead on the paper and wears down more quickly. Every artist has his personal preference, but #2.5 pencils are a good medium grade to start out with until you find your own favorite.

Spend some time drawing with each grade of pencil and get used to their different qualities. Another good product to try is the clutch, or mechanical pencil. These are available in a range of lead thicknesses, 0.5mm being a good medium size. These pencils are very good for fine detail work.

PENS

There is a large range of good quality pens on the market and all will do a decent job of inking. It's important to experiment with a range of different pens to determine which you find most comfortable to work with.

You may find that you end up using a combination of pens to produce your finished piece of artwork. Remember to use a pen that has waterproof ink if you want to color your illustration with a watercolor or ink wash.

It's a good idea to use one of these—there's nothing worse than having your nicely inked drawing ruined by an accidental drop of water!

BRUSHES

Some artists like to use a fine brush for inking linework. This takes a bit more practice and patience to master, but the results can be very satisfying. If you want to try your hand at brushwork, you will definitely need to get some good-quality sable brushes.

ERASER

There are three main types of erasers: rubber, plastic, and putty. Try all three to see which kind you prefer.

PANTONE MARKERS

These are very versatile pens and with practice can give pleasing results.

INKS

With the rise of computers and digital illustration, materials such as inks have become a bit obscure, so you may have to look harder for these, but most good arts and crafts stores should stock them.

WATERCOLORS AND GOUACHE

Most art stores will stock a wide range of these products, from professional to student quality.

CIRCLE TEMPLATE

This is very useful for drawing small circles.

FRENCH CURVES

These are available in a few shapes and sizes and are useful for drawing curves.

BUILDING DINOSAURS

Notice how a simple oval shape forms the body of these three dinosaurs (figs.1, 2, and 3). Even though they are all very differently shaped, an oval forms the body of each one perfectly.

Fig. 4 shows how a dinosaur can be constructed using all these basic shapes. Cylinders are used for its legs and arms, an oval shape forms its body, and a smaller egg shape is used for its head.

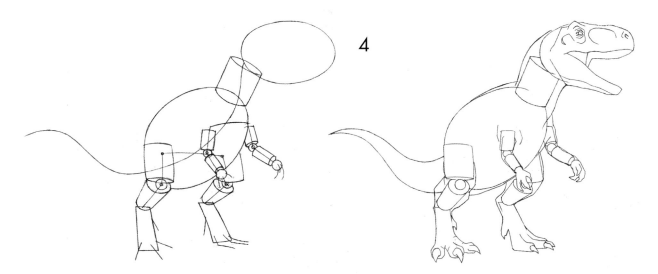

DRAWING THE EYES AND TEETH

Simple circles are all you need to start the eyes (figs. 1 and 2). The appearance of the eye on the face is determined by the construction of the lids (figs. 3 and 4) and the surrounding skin (fig. 5).

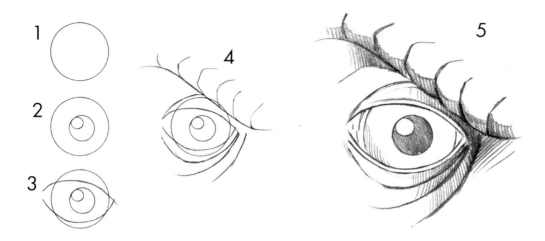

See below to learn how to draw a Velociraptor's eye. Notice that the pupil is similar to that of a cat.

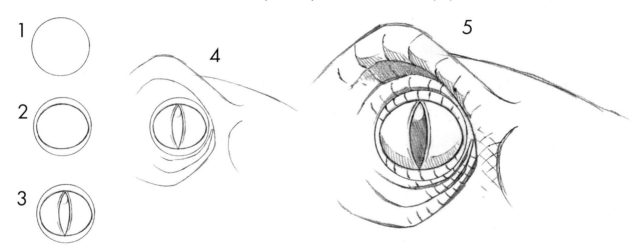

When drawing the teeth, try not to opt for the lazy option of drawing zigzags (fig. 1) but try to think of how animal teeth really look. They come in all shapes and sizes. By taking a bit more time and effort with the teeth, you can give your drawing a more realistic appearance (figs. 2 and 3).

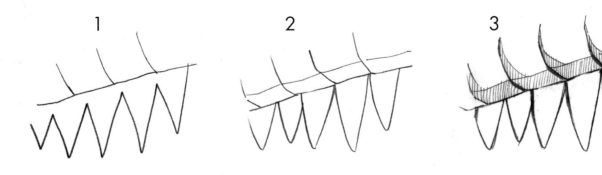

PLESIOSAURUS

DINO FACT FILE

Plesiosaurus was the first plesiosaur to be discovered. Plesiosaurs were a group of marine reptiles with long necks, small heads, and paddle-like flippers. They hatched from eggs buried on sandy shores, like turtles do, but they had crocodile-like teeth and jaws. Specimens have been found with stones in the belly, which they swallowed to help digest food, or to weigh them down for diving.

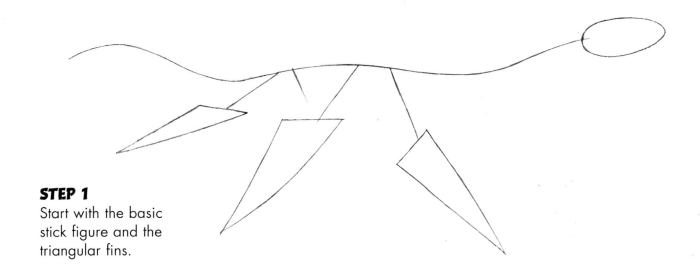

STEP 1
Start with the basic stick figure and the triangular fins.

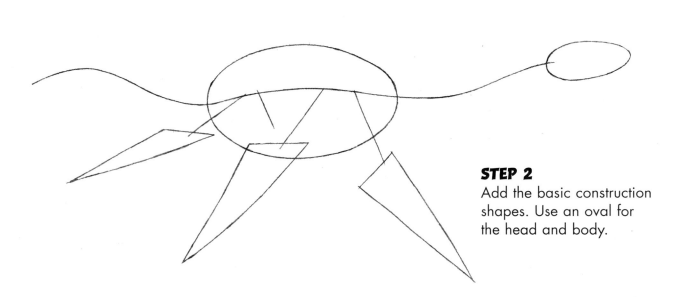

STEP 2
Add the basic construction shapes. Use an oval for the head and body.

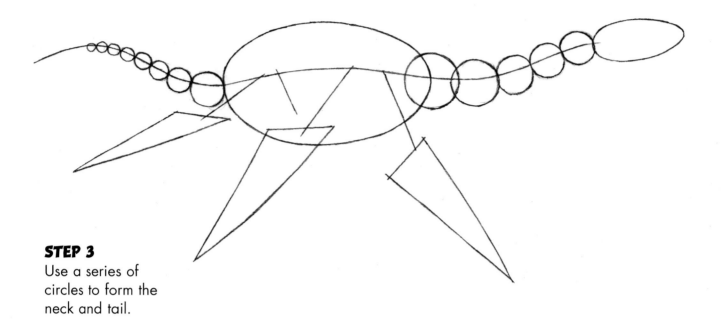

STEP 3

Use a series of circles to form the neck and tail.

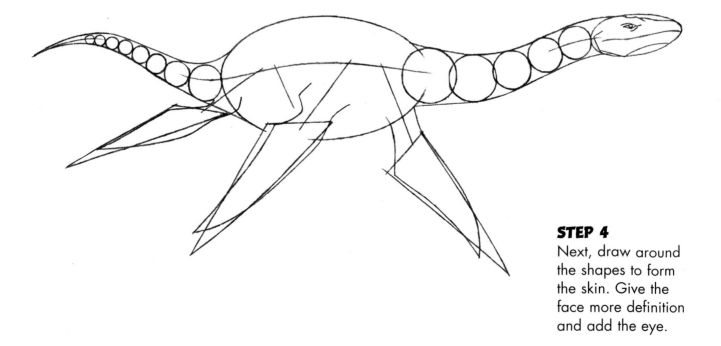

STEP 4

Next, draw around the shapes to form the skin. Give the face more definition and add the eye.

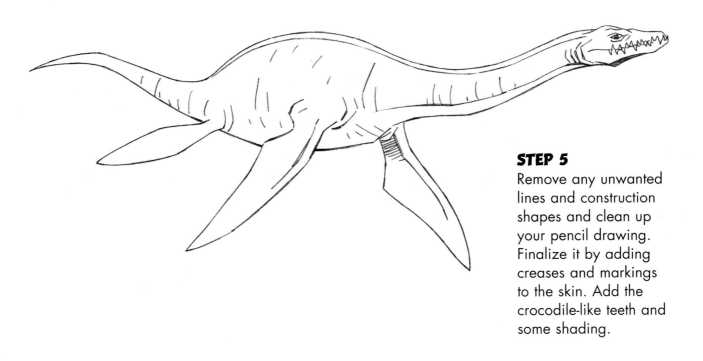

STEP 5

Remove any unwanted lines and construction shapes and clean up your pencil drawing. Finalize it by adding creases and markings to the skin. Add the crocodile-like teeth and some shading.

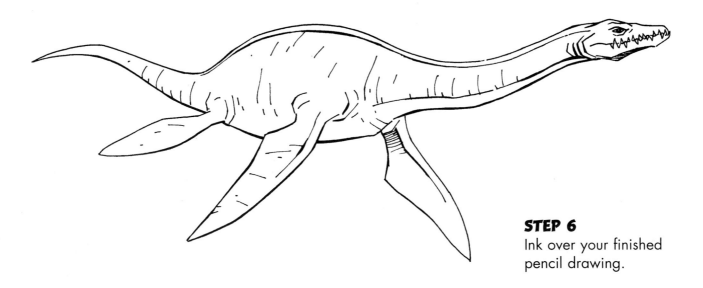

STEP 6

Ink over your finished pencil drawing.

STEP 7

Finally, add color to your Plesiosaurus. Apply a pale gray for the base color. Next apply a very pale aqua over the gray, leaving its belly in the light gray. Over the aqua color add sky blue. Then darken areas of the skin with a midrange blue, leaving areas of the lighter color showing through.

DID YOU KNOW?

ITS LONG NECK MADE PLESIOSAURUS AN EXCELLENT FISH CATCHER. IT WOULD TRAP FISH IN ITS INTERLOCKING TEETH AND SWALLOW THEM WHOLE.

ICHTHYOSAURUS

DINO FACT FILE

Ichthyosaurus was a streamlined dolphin-like marine reptile that could cut throught the water at incredible speeds—up to 25 miles per hour (40 km/h). It lived underwater but still needed to swim to the surface and breathe air. It had huge ear bones and eyes, giving it a keen sense of smell and excellent eyesight. It had lots of sharp teeth and long jaws for snapping up fish to eat.

STEP 1
Start with the basic stick figure.

STEP 2
Add all the basic construction shapes. Use two triangles for the mouth. All the fins are drawn using single triangles and the tail uses two.

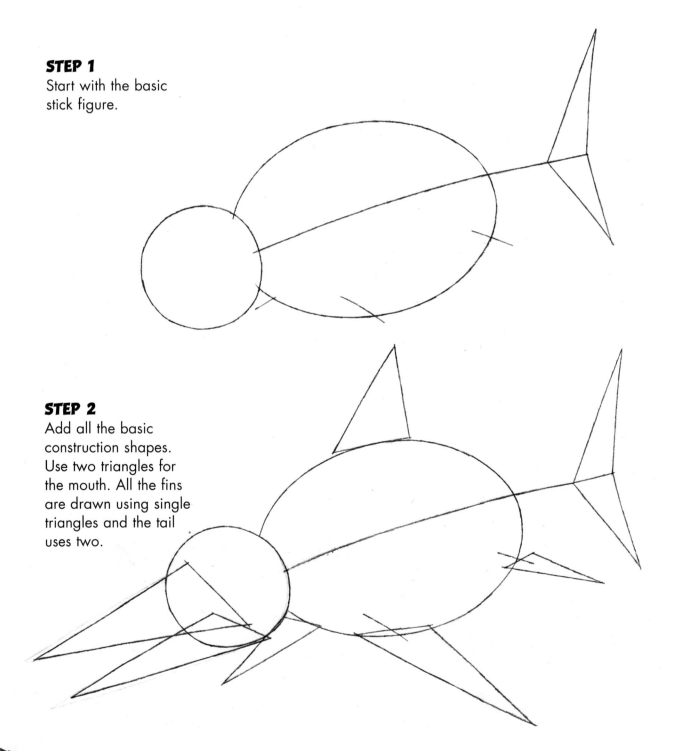

STEP 3
Go around the
construction shapes
to give the body its
proper form. Draw
the large eye.

STEP 4
Remove all your construction
shapes so you have a clean
drawing. Draw in the teeth
and start adding some detail
to the skin.

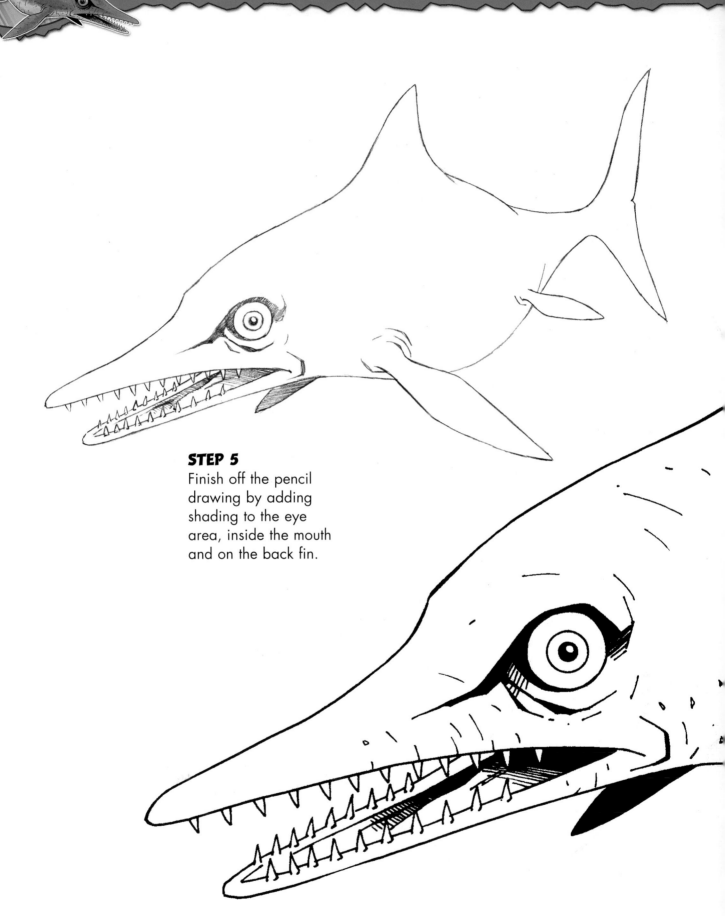

STEP 5
Finish off the pencil drawing by adding shading to the eye area, inside the mouth and on the back fin.

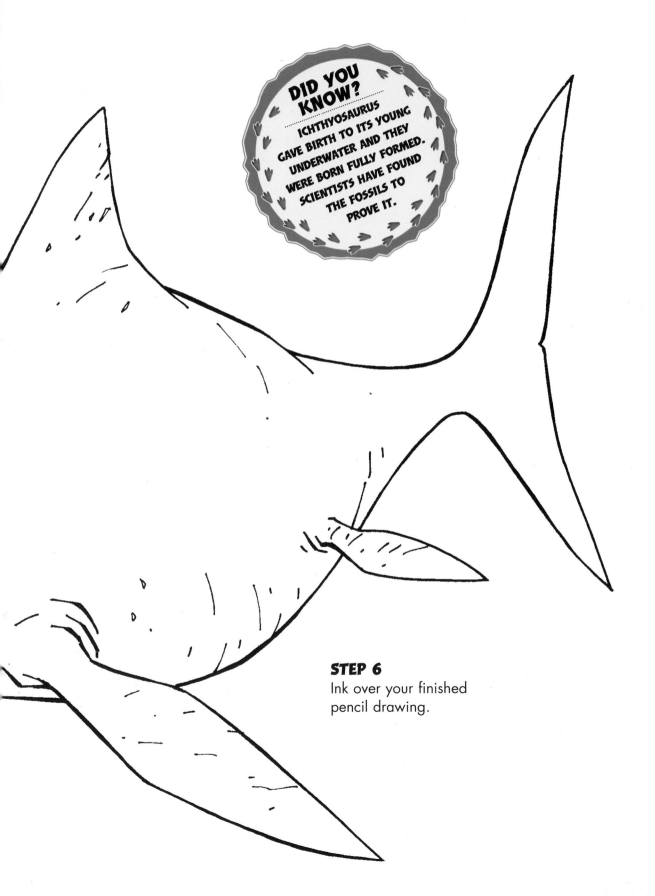

DID YOU KNOW?

ICHTHYOSAURUS GAVE BIRTH TO ITS YOUNG UNDERWATER AND THEY WERE BORN FULLY FORMED. SCIENTISTS HAVE FOUND THE FOSSILS TO PROVE IT.

STEP 6

Ink over your finished pencil drawing.

STEP 7

Now color your drawing. Apply a pale gray for the base color. Apply a very pale aqua over the gray, leaving its belly light gray. Over the aqua color add some sky blue. Then darken areas of the skin with a midrange blue, leaving areas of the lighter color showing through. Finish the drawing by giving Ichthyosaurus a yellow eye.

LIOPLEURODON

DINO FACT FILE

Liopleurodon was a gigantic ocean predator measuring 35 feet (10 m) in length (although some paleontologists think it was much bigger). It was a powerful swimmer with big strong jaws filled with rows of razor-sharp teeth, each one as long as a sword. It sat at the top of the food chain and had no predators, so it cruised the depths with its mouth open, ready to catch its prey.

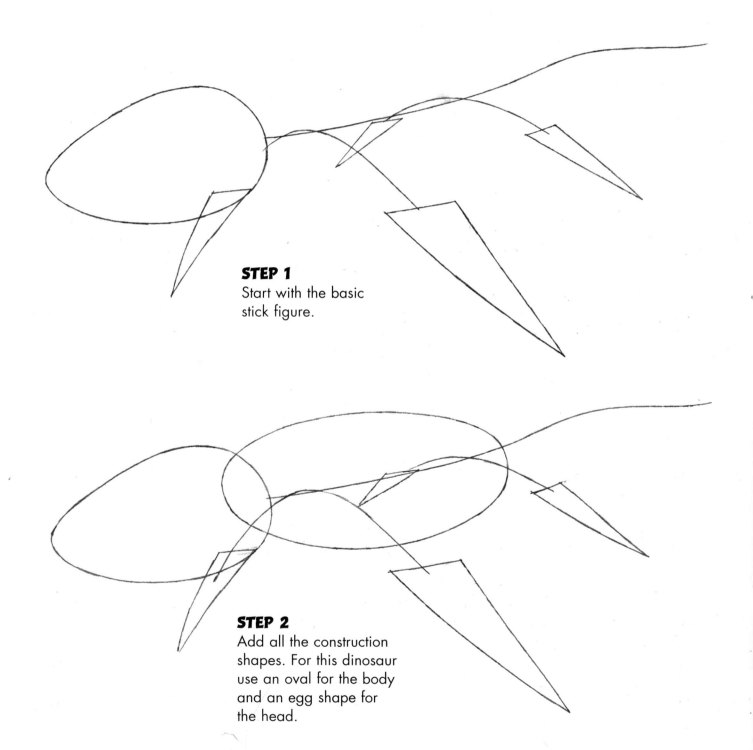

STEP 1

Start with the basic stick figure.

STEP 2

Add all the construction shapes. For this dinosaur use an oval for the body and an egg shape for the head.

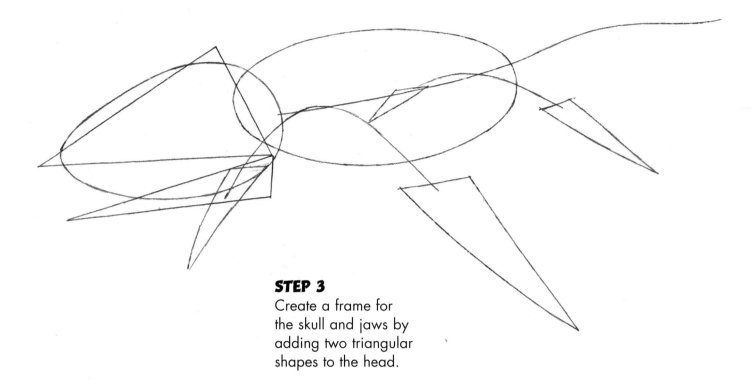

STEP 3

Create a frame for
the skull and jaws by
adding two triangular
shapes to the head.

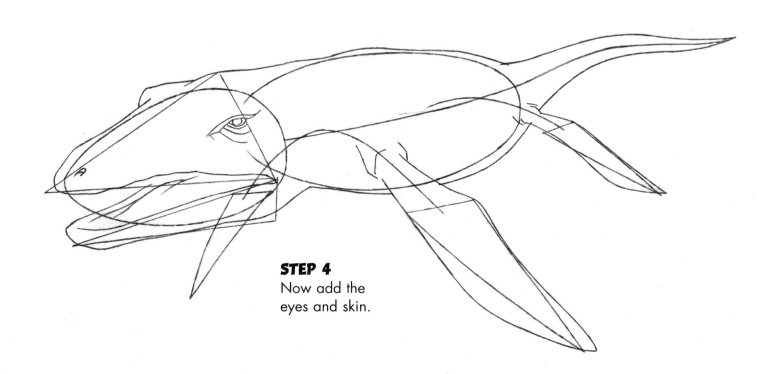

STEP 4

Now add the
eyes and skin.

STEP 5

Finish off your pencil drawing.
Add shading around the eye and
inside the mouth, and develop
more details on the skin.

DID YOU KNOW?
....
LIOPLEURODON WAS ONE OF THE BIGGEST MARINE REPTILES THAT HAS EVER EXISTED. ITS TEETH WERE SO STRONG THEY COULD BITE THROUGH GRANITE.

STEP 6

Now ink over the pencil work. You can add even more details at this stage if you like.

STEP 7

To color Liopleurodon, use pale gray for the base color. Apply midrange gray along its back and tail and along the tops of its fins. Add sky blue on top of this to finish the body. Use pink with gray shading for the tongue.

CREATING A SCENE

OCEAN SCENE FEATURING PLESIOSAURUS

Plesiosaurus survived the mini mass extinction that occurred at the end of the Jurassic period, which killed many marine creatures. It spent all of its time underwater and survived until all dinosaurs died out 65 million years ago. The reason for its success was partly its long neck, which allowed it to trawl along the seabed, gulping up shellfish as well as hunting larger, swimming fish.

STEP 1 Draw a horizon line a quarter of the way up from of the page. On the right, draw a series of curves. Make them bigger and wider in the foreground and smaller and less steep as they go into the distance. Now plot the position of the Plesiosaurus roughly in the center of the page. Draw the basic stick figure (see pages 9–13 for the step-by-step guide).

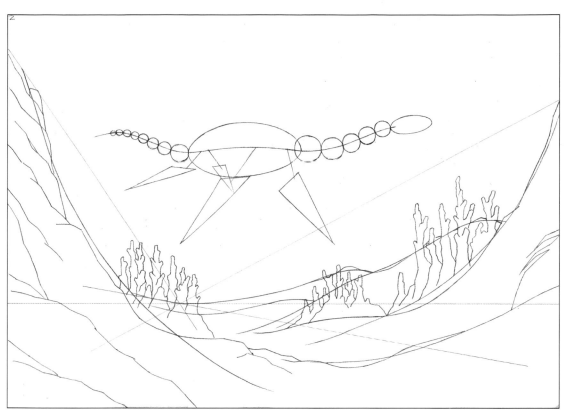

STEP 2 Now add some more detail. Draw lines in the rock on either side and some groups of coral. Add a series of circles for the neck and tail of the Plesiosaurus.

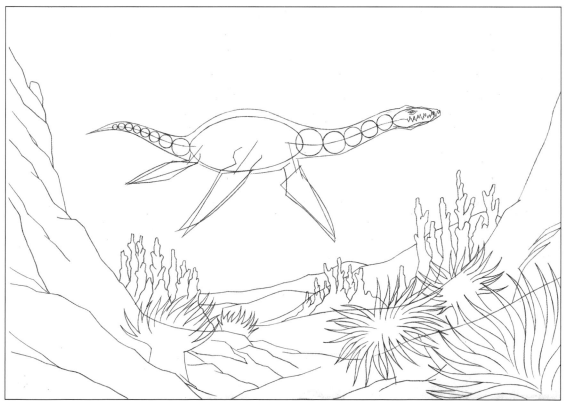

STEP 3 Add some plant life to the seabed. Draw sea anemones in the foreground, varying the sizes to create a sense of depth. Add more detail to the Plesiosaurus.

STEP 4 To finish your pencil drawing, erase any unwanted lines and finalize all the details. Add some shellfish and jellyfish to complete the scene.

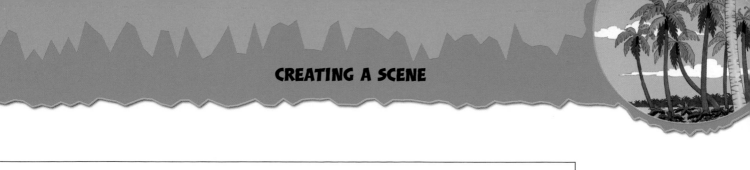

STEP 5 Color your drawing using different shades of aqua for an underwater feel. Some light shining down through the water adds atmosphere.

GLOSSARY

amazing (uh-MAYZ-ing) Wonderful.

cylinders (SIH-len-derz) Shapes with straight sides and circular ends of equal size.

gouache (GWAHSH) A mixture of nontransparent watercolor paint and gum.

mechanical pencil (mih-KA-nih-kul PENT-sul) A pencil with replaceable lead that may be advanced as needed.

reptiles (REP-tylz) Cold-blooded animals with thin, dry pieces of skin called scales.

research (rih-SERCH) Careful study.

structure (STRUK-cher) Form.

watercolor (WAH-ter-kuh-ler) Paint made by mixing pigments (substances that give something its color) with water.

INDEX

WEB SITES

Due to the changing nature of Internet links, PowerKids Press has developed an online list of Web sites related to the subject of this book. This site is updated regularly. Please use this link to access the list: www.powerkidslinks.com/ddino/plesiosaurus/